Mixes
in Jars
For Kids!

Original Mixes For Gifts
Jackie Gannaway

Published in Austin, TX by COOKBOOK CUPBOARD P.O. Box 50053, Austin, TX 78763   (512) 477-7070 phone   (512) 891-0094 fax

Artwork by Frank Bielec of Mosey 'N Me - Katy, TX

This book is part of the Layers of Love™ Collection from Cookbook Cupboard. This collection consists of 9 booklets about layering mixes in jars for gifts. All rights reserved.

Over 1.5 Million Copies Of Jackie Gannaway's Books Are In Print!

Kitchen Crafts Collection

Jackie Gannaway

ORDER OUR 40 BOOK TITLES FROM COOKBOOKCUPBOARD.COM

Mail Order Information

To order a copy of this book send a check for $3.95 + $1.50 for shipping (TX residents add 8.25 % sales tax) to Cookbook Cupboard, P.O. Box 50053, Austin, TX 78763. Send a note asking for this title by name.

If you would like a descriptive list of the 40 fun titles in The Kitchen Crafts Collection, send a note, call, or fax asking for an order blank.   Phone 512 477-7070   Fax 512 891-0094

What Is This Book About?

This book is the ninth in The Layers of Love™ Collection from Cookbook Cupboard. Each book in that collection is about layering mixes in jars for gifts.

All the dry ingredients are packed tightly in layers in a "wide-mouth" canning jar - the lid of the jar is decorated and instructions are attached telling the recipient how to make the finished food.

These make perfect gifts because they require no cooking on the part of the person filling the jar.

The jars keep several months so they can be made well ahead of the holiday or event.

They are inexpensive to make - especially for the amount of pleasure they bring. They are also easy for the recipient because almost everything they need has been bought and measured for them!.

This book has recipes of special interest to kids - they can help make the mixes as gifts and when a child receives a mix as a gift - he can help make the finished food.

Some of these recipes can be made by the recipient and THEN GIVEN AWAY as a further gift. Example - Give the teacher a chocolate fudge mix in a jar - she makes it with her personal children and then they give the actual fudge pieces to their grandmother with the pride of having made the fudge themselves.

How To Read The Format Of This Book And Copyright Information

Each recipe is complete on 1 page. The top of the page lists the ingredients and the order to put them into the jar.

The bottom of the page has instructions to attach to the jar so the recipient knows how to make the food.

What Kind Of Jars To Use

Canning jars can be purchased at grocery stores (they will order the size you need in 3-4 days if they don't have it in stock). Jars are also available at hardware stores and "dollar" stores. Discount stores have them in stock during the summer (canning season). The simplest thing is to ask your grocery store to get them for you. They come in a case of 12 with lids. If you have some used canning jars you can use them for these mixes- the grocery store sells lids in a small pack separately.

You need the "wide-mouth" jar style so you can get your hand inside the jar to <u>very tightly pack</u> the ingredients.

The 3 sizes used in this book are quart, pint and half-pint. They are clearly labeled as to size and "wide-mouth" on the box. The half-pint (8 oz.) jar comes in two shapes - short and tall. The short one is best because you can get your hand in the opening.

Peanut Butter Jars: 18 oz. peanut butter jars can be used in place of the pint jars in these recipes - they are hard to get your hand in - but kids will be able to get their hands in the peanut butter jars. You can save peanut butter jars throughout the year. They are plastic which is also good for kids as compared to glass jars.

How To Layer The Ingredients

Each ingredient is placed in the jar in the order listed at the top of the page. The first ingredient listed is the first thing placed in the jar. Each ingredient needs to be leveled and packed AS TIGHTLY AS YOU POSSIBLY CAN. This is important because loosely packed jars will "mix up" with the very slightest handling. Just carrying them in your car can cause the ingredients to be unrecognizable when you get to your destination if they are not tightly packed.

Attaching Instructions To Jars

Copy the instructions from the bottom of the page onto a recipe card. Tape that onto the front of the jar or hang it by ribbon from the top of the jar. Personalize by adding stickers, clip art from your computer, rubber stamp designs, your own art work.

Zipper Baggies

Many recipes in this book require the ingredients to be kept separate for the final cooking. That is done by putting some of the ingredients in a zipper baggie (sandwich bag size) and then putting the baggie into the jar.

After putting the ingredient into the baggie, unzip 1" and let out the air. Then put the bag into the jar.

If it goes in the middle of the jar pack it in very flat and tight with your hands. If it goes into the jar last, just push and squeeze it forcefully until it is all inside the jar. You can use the lid of the jar to give it that final push to get it all inside the jar.

Decorating The Jar Lids

The jars can be decorated by cutting a circle of fabric, brown paper sack or wrapping paper and covering the lid with that. Hold that in place with a rubber band and then tie on a ribbon or raffia bow.

This is a perfect way for the kids to use their art ability. They can draw on brown paper sacks or butcher paper for the jar toppers. You can buy craft paint that is suitable for painting on glass. Let the kids paint designs on the jars and coordinate that art design with the jar topper.

Some of the recipes in this book lend themselves to a particular theme (Circus Parade Cake, Birthday Cupcakes, Puppy Chow for People, Dog Treats). Fabric is available in all those themes.

Also you can glue on small objects from the crafts store to add interest to the jar lid. You can even make or buy a Christmas ornament or other small gift and attach it to the jar for a double gift.

Ordering Other Books

We can sell you the other books in the Layers of Love™ Collection. Our address and phone number is on the copyright page of this book.

5

Mix For Dog Treats in a Pint Jar

3/4 cup whole wheat flour
1/3 cup powdered milk
Mix the following 4 ingredients -place in jar next:
    1/4 tsp. salt
    1/2 tsp. garlic powder
    2 tsp. brown sugar
    2 tsp. beef bouillon granules
3/4 cup more whole wheat flour
cookie cutter to tie onto jar (optional)

    Layer ingredients in order given in a 1 pint "wide mouth" canning jar. Press each layer firmly in place. Use a skewer to push up and down against the inside glass of the jar to make a spiked "sand-art" design if desired.

    Top jar with more flour (because the ingredients will have settled somewhat.) Tie on a dog bone (or other shape) cookie cutter. Give with instructions below.
See pgs. 4-5 for detailed instructions on layering and decorating jars.

Dog Treats

1. Empty contents of jar into a medium bowl. Blend dry ingredients.
2. Add: 1 egg
           1/2 cup water
           1/4 cup oil or bacon drippings
3. Mix well.
4. Roll out to 1/2" thickness. Cut into shapes with cookie cutters. Place on sprayed baking sheet. Bake at 350° for 20 to 25 minutes.

Puppy Chow For People Mix in a Quart Jar

1/2 cup chocolate chips
3/4 cup powdered sugar in a zipper baggie
3 cups Crispix® cereal

Place chips in a "wide-mouth" quart canning jar. Then push bag of powdered sugar into bag very firmly so it lays evenly on top of chips. Put cereal into jar 1 cup at a time, tapping jar on counter to settle cereal, If you can't get all the cereal into the jar, remove cereal and flatten the zipper bag of powdered sugar even flatter than it was. Then put in the cereal. Give with instructions below.
See pgs. 4-5 for detailed instructions on layering and decorating jars.

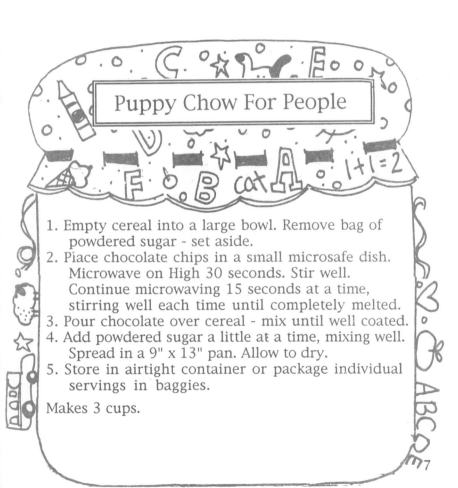

Puppy Chow For People

1. Empty cereal into a large bowl. Remove bag of powdered sugar - set aside.
2. Place chocolate chips in a small microsafe dish. Microwave on High 30 seconds. Stir well. Continue microwaving 15 seconds at a time, stirring well each time until completely melted.
3. Pour chocolate over cereal - mix until well coated.
4. Add powdered sugar a little at a time, mixing well. Spread in a 9" x 13" pan. Allow to dry.
5. Store in airtight container or package individual servings in baggies.

Makes 3 cups.

Candy Corn Crispy Treats
Mix in a Quart Jar

1/2 cup peanut butter chips (like choc. chips, but peanut butter flavored)
1/2 cup candy corn
1 3/4 cups crisp rice cereal
16 marshmallows placed in a zipper baggie

Layer ingredients in order given in a 1 quart "wide mouth" canning jar. Press each layer firmly in place. Unzip 1" of the marshmallow bag to let out air.

Press this bag very hard to get it all the way into the jar. Give with instructions below.

See pgs. 4-5 for detailed instructions on layering and decorating jars.

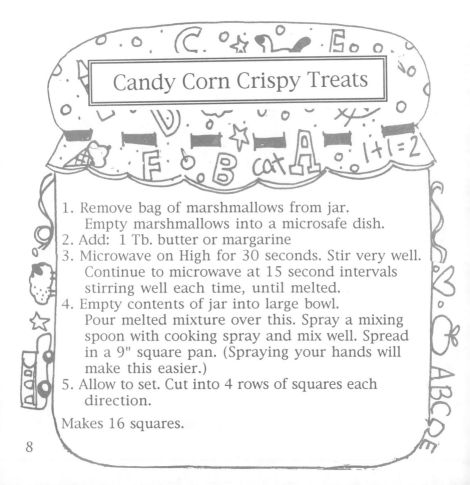

Candy Corn Crispy Treats

1. Remove bag of marshmallows from jar.
   Empty marshmallows into a microsafe dish.
2. Add: 1 Tb. butter or margarine
3. Microwave on High for 30 seconds. Stir very well.
   Continue to microwave at 15 second intervals stirring well each time, until melted.
4. Empty contents of jar into large bowl.
   Pour melted mixture over this. Spray a mixing spoon with cooking spray and mix well. Spread in a 9" square pan. (Spraying your hands will make this easier.)
5. Allow to set. Cut into 4 rows of squares each direction.

Makes 16 squares.

Crispy Treat Mix in a Quart Jar

2 1/2 cups crisp rice cereal
2 cups mini marshmallows in a zipper baggie.

Layer ingredients in order given in a 1 quart "wide mouth" canning jar. Press each layer firmly in place. Give with instructions below.

See pgs. 4-5 for detailed instructions on layering and decorating jars.

Crispy Treats

1. Place marshmallows in a large microsafe dish.
   Add: 1/4 stick butter or margarine
2. Microwave on High 1 minute. Stir well.
   If not completely melted microwave 20
   seconds more. Stir well.
3. Add cereal to melted mixture and stir well.
4. Spread mixture into a sprayed 8" or 9" square pan
   (Spraying your hands will help spread mix.)
5. Allow to set. Cut into 4 rows of squares in each
   direction.

Makes 16 squares.

Crunchy Peanut Butter Cookie
Mix in a Pint Jar

1/4 cup honey roasted peanuts
1/2 cup peanut butter chips (like choc. chips, but peanut
   butter flavored)
1 3/4 cup yellow cake mix (this is half a cake mix)

   Layer ingredients in order given in a 1 pint "wide mouth" canning jar. Press each layer firmly in place. Give with instructions below.
See pgs. 4-5 for detailed instructions on layering and decorating jars.

Crunchy Peanut Butter Cookies

1. Empty contents of jar into a medium bowl.
   Blend dry ingredients.
2. Add: 1 egg
         1/4 cup oil
3. Mix well. Shape into walnut-sized balls.
   Place 2" apart on sprayed baking sheets.
4. Bake at 350° for 12 to 15 minutes. Cool
   3 minutes on baking sheet. Remove to
   wire rack to finish cooling.

Makes 18 cookies.

Peanut Butter Cookie Mix in a Quart Jar

1 yellow cake mix
1/3 cup sugar placed in a zipper baggie
24 Hersheys® kisses, unwrapped and placed in a baggie
    Note - if you are using any of the holiday Hershey's
    Kisses, leave them wrapped so the colors can show
    through the jar.

Place cake mix into a "wide-mouth" quart jar, pressing
in lightly at first. Place bag of sugar flat on top of cake mix.
Then place baggie of candy in jar. (You want the cake mix
to only be pressed in far enough to accommodate the bag of
candy.) Give with instructions below.
See pgs. 4-5 for detailed instructions on layering and decorating jars.

Peanut Butter Cookies

1. Remove bag of candy from jar. Set aside.
2. Empty jar into large bowl.
3. Add: 2 eggs
            1 cup peanut butter, smooth or crunchy
            1/3 cup water
4. Mix well with electric mixer.
5. Shape into 24 balls a little bigger than walnuts.
   Place these on a sprayed baking sheet.
6. Empty the bag of sugar into a saucer. Dip a fork
   in this sugar and make a criss-cross design on
   top of each cookie, flattening the dough. Re-dip
   fork in sugar each time.
7. Bake at 375° for 12 -15 minutes.
8. Immediately place an unwrapped candy kiss on
   top of each cookie. Let cookies cool 5 minutes
   on baking sheet.

Makes 24 cookies.

Gum Drop Cookie Mix in a Pint Jar

1 3/4 cup white cake mix (this is half a cake mix)
1/2 cup gum drops, cut in half and tossed in:
2 tsp. sugar (so they won't be sticky)

   Layer ingredients in order given in a 1 pint "wide mouth" canning jar. Press each layer firmly in place. Give with instructions below.

See pgs. 4-5 for detailed instructions on layering and decorating jars.

Gum Drop Cookies

1. Empty jar into a medium bowl. Mix well.
2. Add: 1 eggwhite
           1/4 cup oil
3. Mix until completely blended.
4. Shape into walnut sized balls.
   Place 2" apart on a sprayed baking sheet.
5. Bake at 350° for 12 to 15 minutes.

Makes 18 cookies.

Dirt Pudding Mix With Worms
in a Pint Jar

8 long gummy "worms" candies
1 (4-serving) box instant chocolate pudding (not sugar
    free)
8 Oreo® cookies - place in a zipper baggie and crush with a
    rolling pin or a food can. Leave crushed cookies in bag.
4 (8 to 10 oz.) clear plastic cups

Use a 1 pint "wide-mouth" canning jar. Put worms in first. Flatten them out in bottom of jar. Add loose pudding mix next - press in very firmly.

Top with baggie of crushed cookies. Turn cups upside down and attach to top of jar with tape. Decorate jar if desired, using a much larger circle of paper or fabric to cover cups. Give with instructions below.

See pgs. 4-5 for detailed instructions on layering and decorating jars.

Dirt Pudding With Worms

1. Remove bag of crushed cookies from jar.
   Set aside.
2. Empty jar into a large mixing bowl. Remove
   worms and set them aside.
3. Add: 2 cups milk
4. Mix well. Place in refrigerator to set.
5. When set, divide pudding among 4 plastic cups.
6. Top each pudding cup with some of the crushed
   cookies and with 2 worms.

Microwave Peanut Butter Fudge Mix in a Quart Jar

1/2 cup chopped peanuts
1 (10-12 oz.) pkg. peanut butter chips (like chocolate chips,
    but peanut butter flavored (1 3/4 to 2 cups chips)
3 cups mini marshmallows

Layer ingredients in order given in a 1 quart "wide mouth" canning jar. Press each layer firmly in place.

It will be hard to get all the marshmallows into the jar, but they do fit. Give with instructions below.

See pgs. 4-5 for detailed instructions on layering and decorating jars.

Microwave Peanut Butter Fudge

1. Spray a 9" x 13" pan with cooking spray. Set aside.
2. Empty contents of jar into very large bowl.
3. Add: 1 stick margarine or butter, cut into 6 pieces.
4. Into a very large, deep microsafe dish place:
    3 cups sugar
    1 (5 oz.) can evaporated milk

    Stir until well mixed. Cover with plastic wrap, turning back a corner to vent heat. Microwave on High 4 minutes. Stir well, re-cover. Continue to microwave 1 minute at a time until mixture comes to a boil - (2 to 4 minutes).

    When it comes to a boil, allow to boil 1 minute. Use hot pad to remove dish from microwave.
5. Pour hot mixture into marshmallow mixture.

    Stir rapidly for 2 minutes to melt marshmallows. Pour into sprayed 9" x 13" pan to cool. Chill up to 4 hours to set firmly. Cut into 1 1/2" squares. Store in refrigerator.

Makes 48 pieces.

Microwave Chocolate Fudge Mix in a Quart Jar

1/2 cup chopped pecans
1 (12 oz.) pkg. chocolate chips (2 cups)
3 cups mini marshmallows

Layer ingredients in order given in a 1 quart "wide mouth" canning jar. Press each layer firmly in place.

It will be hard to get all the marshmallows into the jar, but they do fit. Give with instructions below.

See pgs. 4-5 for detailed instructions on layering and decorating jars.

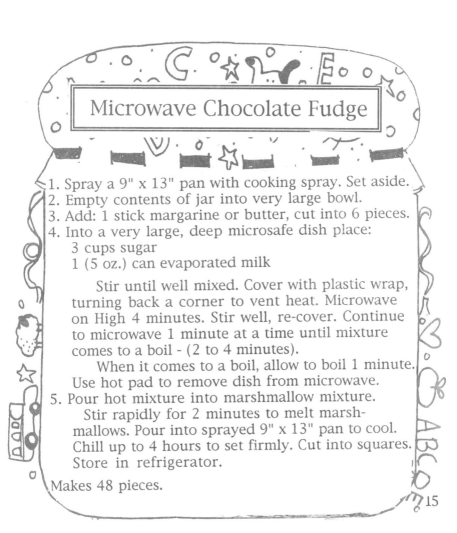

Microwave Chocolate Fudge

1. Spray a 9" x 13" pan with cooking spray. Set aside.
2. Empty contents of jar into very large bowl.
3. Add: 1 stick margarine or butter, cut into 6 pieces.
4. Into a very large, deep microsafe dish place:
   3 cups sugar
   1 (5 oz.) can evaporated milk

   Stir until well mixed. Cover with plastic wrap, turning back a corner to vent heat. Microwave on High 4 minutes. Stir well, re-cover. Continue to microwave 1 minute at a time until mixture comes to a boil - (2 to 4 minutes).

   When it comes to a boil, allow to boil 1 minute. Use hot pad to remove dish from microwave.
5. Pour hot mixture into marshmallow mixture.

   Stir rapidly for 2 minutes to melt marshmallows. Pour into sprayed 9" x 13" pan to cool. Chill up to 4 hours to set firmly. Cut into squares. Store in refrigerator.

Makes 48 pieces.

15

Birthday Cupcake Mix In A Quart Jar

1 cake mix, any flavor
2 Tb. colored sprinkles in a zipper baggie
1 unwrapped Hershey's Kiss® or similar chocolate candy
1 1/2 cups powdered sugar placed in a zipper baggie - label
    this "Glaze Mix"
1 box of 24 birthday candles
24 tiny (1 1/2") balloons in a zipper baggie

Place cake mix into jar. Press down very firmly.
Put chocolate kiss in baggie with sprinkles. Place baggie of
sprinkles in jar on top of cake mix - flatten out baggie so
sprinkles show from all sides of jar.

Put baggie of powdered sugar into jar last, pressing in
very firmly until it all fits into jar.

The box of candles probably have a hole in the top - fold
baggie of balloons in half so it is the same width as the box
of candles. Place candles at the top of the balloon baggie, so
balloons are visible beneath the candles. Punch a hole in
top of baggie - use that hole and the hole in the candle box
to attach these two items onto outside of the jar with a
ribbon. Put lid on jar.

Read the cake mix box and adjust eggs, oil and water on
facing page if necessary to match the type of cake mix you
are using. Give with instructions on facing page.

See pgs. 4-5 for detailed instructions on layering and decorating jars.

Instructions for this recipe on pg. 17.

This recipe continued from pg. 16.

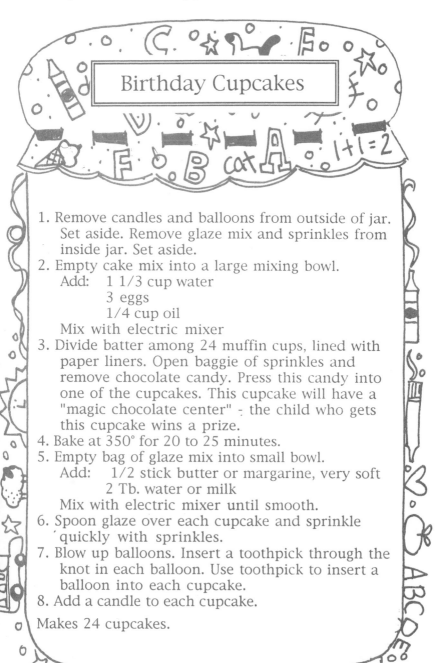

Birthday Cupcakes

1. Remove candles and balloons from outside of jar. Set aside. Remove glaze mix and sprinkles from inside jar. Set aside.
2. Empty cake mix into a large mixing bowl.
   Add: 1 1/3 cup water
          3 eggs
          1/4 cup oil
   Mix with electric mixer
3. Divide batter among 24 muffin cups, lined with paper liners. Open baggie of sprinkles and remove chocolate candy. Press this candy into one of the cupcakes. This cupcake will have a "magic chocolate center" - the child who gets this cupcake wins a prize.
4. Bake at 350° for 20 to 25 minutes.
5. Empty bag of glaze mix into small bowl.
   Add: 1/2 stick butter or margarine, very soft
          2 Tb. water or milk
   Mix with electric mixer until smooth.
6. Spoon glaze over each cupcake and sprinkle quickly with sprinkles.
7. Blow up balloons. Insert a toothpick through the knot in each balloon. Use toothpick to insert a balloon into each cupcake.
8. Add a candle to each cupcake.

Makes 24 cupcakes.

Fortune Cupcake Mix In A Quart Jar

1 cake mix, any flavor
2 Tb. colored sprinkles placed in a zipper baggie
1 1/2 cups powdered sugar placed in a zipper baggie - label
  this "Glaze Mix"
24 pieces of index card cut to 1 1/4" x 1 1/4" with a hole
  punched near one end of each piece
24 6" pieces of curling ribbon

Place cake mix into jar. Press down very firmly. Place baggie
of sprinkles into jar on top of cake mix - flatten out baggie so
sprinkles show from all sides of jar.

Place glaze mix baggie into jar last, pressing in very firmly.

Place index cards and ribbons into a baggie - tie onto outside of
the jar. Read cake mix box - adjust eggs, oil and water below if
needed to match cake mix you are using. Attach instructions below.
See pgs. 4-5 for detailed instructions on layering and decorating jars.

Fortune Cupcakes

1. Remove baggie of ribbons - set aside. Remove
   glaze mix and sprinkles from jar - set aside.
2. Empty cake mix into a large mixing bowl.
   Add: 1 1/3 cup water
             3 eggs
             1/4 cup oil - Mix with electric mixer.
3. Divide batter among 24 paper lined muffin cups.
4. Bake at 350° for 20 to 25 minutes.
5. Empty bag of glaze mix into small bowl.
   Add: 1/2 stick butter or margarine, very soft
             2 Tb. water or milk.
   Mix with electric mixer until smooth.
6. Spoon glaze over each cupcake and sprinkle
   quickly with sprinkles.
7. Write a "fortune" on each little card. Wrap each
   card with foil and tie a ribbon through the hole
   punch in each card. Curl ends of the ribbon.
8. Carefully slip a fortune into each cupcake with
   ribbon completely outside cupcake. The ribbon
   is pulled to remove fortune from cupcake.

18
                    Makes 24 cupcakes.

Circus Parade Cake Mix In A Quart Jar

9 Keebler® spring colors vanilla wafers

9 animal crackers, plain or frosted

1/4 cup flaked coconut (tint with green food color to make
  grass) - place this in a zipper baggie

1 3/4 cup any flavor cake mix (this is half a cake mix) -
  put cake mix in a zipper baggie. Label this "Cake Mix".

1 1/2 cups powdered sugar placed in a zipper baggie - label
  this "Glaze Mix"

  Layer ingredients in order given in a 1 quart "wide
mouth" canning jar. Press each baggie firmly in place.
(Arrange the coconut flat in the bag and fold excess bag
underneath.) Give with instructions below.
See pgs. 4-5 for detailed instructions on layering and decorating jars.

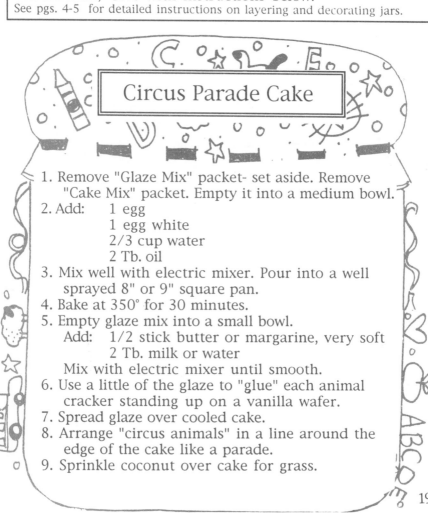

Circus Parade Cake

1. Remove "Glaze Mix" packet- set aside. Remove
   "Cake Mix" packet. Empty it into a medium bowl.
2. Add: 1 egg
           1 egg white
           2/3 cup water
           2 Tb. oil
3. Mix well with electric mixer. Pour into a well
   sprayed 8" or 9" square pan.
4. Bake at 350° for 30 minutes.
5. Empty glaze mix into a small bowl.
     Add: 1/2 stick butter or margarine, very soft
             2 Tb. milk or water
   Mix with electric mixer until smooth.
6. Use a little of the glaze to "glue" each animal
   cracker standing up on a vanilla wafer.
7. Spread glaze over cooled cake.
8. Arrange "circus animals" in a line around the
   edge of the cake like a parade.
9. Sprinkle coconut over cake for grass.

19

Earthquake Cake Mix in a Quart Jar

1/2 cup flaked coconut
1/2 cup chopped nuts
1 3/4 cups German chocolate cake mix (this is half a cake
    mix). Place into a zipper baggie and label it "Cake Mix"
2 cups powdered sugar placed into a zipper baggie
    and labeled "Powdered Sugar"

Layer ingredients in order given in a 1 quart "wide
mouth" canning jar. Press each layer very firmly in place.
Give with instructions below - changing amount of eggs,
oil, water if necessary to match brand of cake mix you used.
See pgs. 4-5 for detailed instructions on layering and decorating jars.

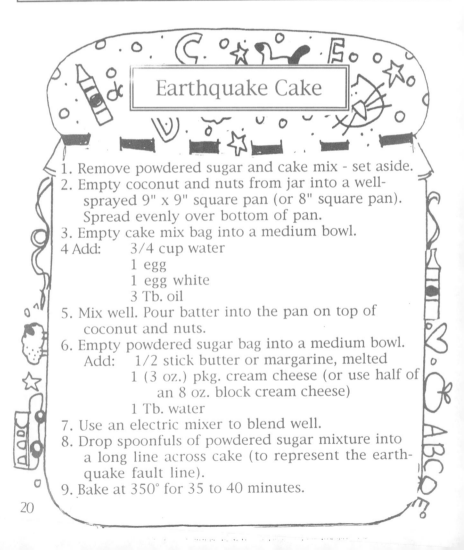

Earthquake Cake

1. Remove powdered sugar and cake mix - set aside.
2. Empty coconut and nuts from jar into a well-
      sprayed 9" x 9" square pan (or 8" square pan).
      Spread evenly over bottom of pan.
3. Empty cake mix bag into a medium bowl.
4. Add: 3/4 cup water
            1 egg
            1 egg white
            3 Tb. oil
5. Mix well. Pour batter into the pan on top of
      coconut and nuts.
6. Empty powdered sugar bag into a medium bowl.
      Add: 1/2 stick butter or margarine, melted
             1 (3 oz.) pkg. cream cheese (or use half of
                 an 8 oz. block cream cheese)
             1 Tb. water
7. Use an electric mixer to blend well.
8. Drop spoonfuls of powdered sugar mixture into
      a long line across cake (to represent the earth-
      quake fault line).
9. Bake at 350° for 35 to 40 minutes.

Ice Cream Frosty Mix
in a Half Pint Jar - 2 Flavors

1/2 cup chopped Reese's Peanut Butter Cups® OR
  1/2 cup crushed Oreo® cookies

1/2 cup Reese's Pieces® candies OR
  1/2 cup M and M's® candies

Note: Choose which <u>one</u> to make - <u>either</u> the Reese's one OR the Oreo/M and M's one. You can also make up your own favorite flavor - it looks best in the jar to have 2 completely different items that are compatible in flavor - the jar wouldn't look as interesting if it was only filled with crushed Oreos for example.

Use a half pint "wide-mouth" canning jar for this recipe (this jar holds 8 oz.) Place first ingredient in jar first. Then fill jar with second ingredient allowing some of second ingredient to fall into any gaps in bottom of jar. Give with instructions below. The instructions work with any flavor.

See pgs. 4-5 for detailed instructions on layering and decorating jars.

Ice Cream Frosty

1. Place 1 quart (4 cups) of vanilla ice cream (or frozen yogurt) into a blender.
2. Add 1/2 cup milk.
3. Empty contents of jar into blender.
4. Blend on High, stopping to stir as necessary. Blend until completely blended and creamy. Serve immediately.

Makes 2 to 4 servings.

Salt Dough Ornament Mix in a Pint Jar

1/3 cup salt mixed with:
1 Tb. powdered tempera paint of desired color
1 3/4 cup flour
cookie cutter(s) to tie onto jar (optional)

Layer ingredients in order given in a 1 pint "wide mouth" canning jar. Press each layer firmly in place. Tie cookie cutters onto jar. Give with instructions below.
See pgs. 4-5 for detailed instructions on layering and decorating jars.

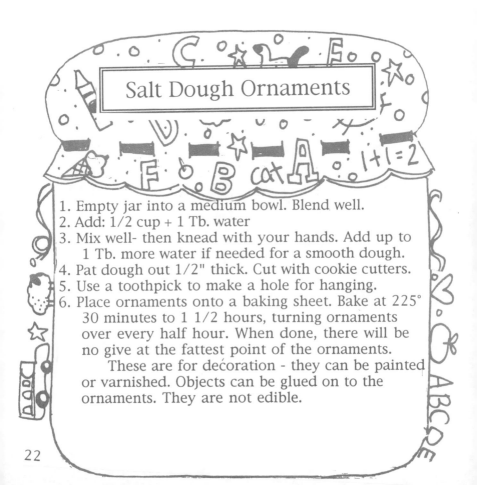

Salt Dough Ornaments

1. Empty jar into a medium bowl. Blend well.
2. Add: 1/2 cup + 1 Tb. water
3. Mix well- then knead with your hands. Add up to 1 Tb. more water if needed for a smooth dough.
4. Pat dough out 1/2" thick. Cut with cookie cutters.
5. Use a toothpick to make a hole for hanging.
6. Place ornaments onto a baking sheet. Bake at 225° 30 minutes to 1 1/2 hours, turning ornaments over every half hour. When done, there will be no give at the fattest point of the ornaments.

These are for decoration - they can be painted or varnished. Objects can be glued on to the ornaments. They are not edible.

Cinnamon Salt Dough Ornament Mix in a Half Pint Jar

3 Tb. salt
1/4 cup cinnamon (buy in bulk at places like Sam's Club)
1/2 cup flour
cookie cutter(s) to tie onto jar (optional)

Layer ingredients in order given in a 1/2 pint "wide mouth" canning jar (this is a jar that holds 8 oz.).
Press each layer firmly in place.

Tie on one or more cookie cutters, if desired. Give with instructions below.

See pgs. 4-5 for detailed instructions on layering and decorating jars.

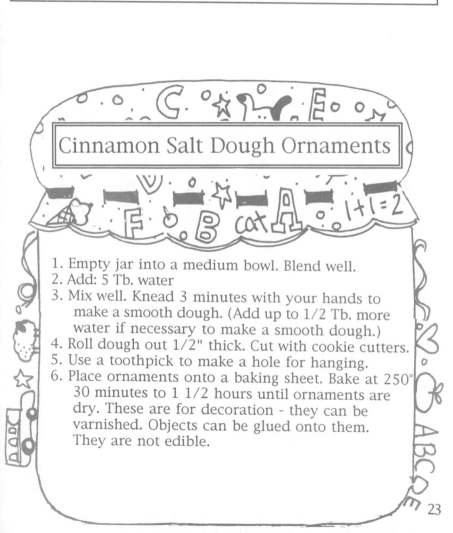

Cinnamon Salt Dough Ornaments

1. Empty jar into a medium bowl. Blend well.
2. Add: 5 Tb. water
3. Mix well. Knead 3 minutes with your hands to make a smooth dough. (Add up to 1/2 Tb. more water if necessary to make a smooth dough.)
4. Roll dough out 1/2" thick. Cut with cookie cutters.
5. Use a toothpick to make a hole for hanging.
6. Place ornaments onto a baking sheet. Bake at 250° 30 minutes to 1 1/2 hours until ornaments are dry. These are for decoration - they can be varnished. Objects can be glued onto them. They are not edible.

23

Fudge With A Crunch
Mix in a Quart Jar

3/4 cup chocolate chips
3/4 cup butterscotch chips (like choc. chips but butter-
    scotch flavor)
1 1/2 cups chow mein noodles placed in a zipper baggie
1 cup graham cracker crumbs placed in a zipper baggie
    (buy a box of graham crumbs)

Layer ingredients in order given in a 1 quart "wide mouth" canning jar. Press each layer firmly in place. Give with instructions below.

See pgs. 4-5 for detailed instructions on layering and decorating jars.

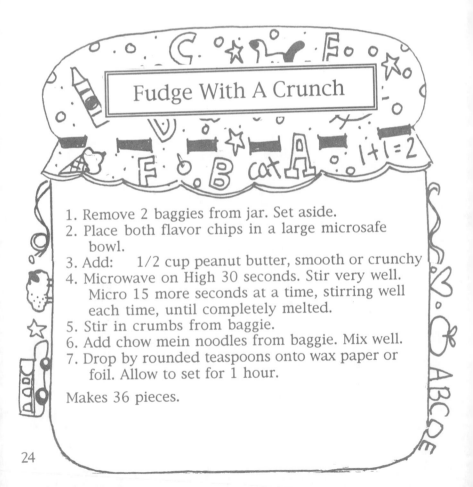

Fudge With A Crunch

1. Remove 2 baggies from jar. Set aside.
2. Place both flavor chips in a large microsafe bowl.
3. Add: 1/2 cup peanut butter, smooth or crunchy
4. Microwave on High 30 seconds. Stir very well. Micro 15 more seconds at a time, stirring well each time, until completely melted.
5. Stir in crumbs from baggie.
6. Add chow mein noodles from baggie. Mix well.
7. Drop by rounded teaspoons onto wax paper or foil. Allow to set for 1 hour.

Makes 36 pieces.

Chocolate Peanut Butter Candy Mix in a Quart Jar

(These taste like Reese's Peanut Butter Cups®)

2/3 cup graham cracker crumbs (buy a box of crumbs)
1 3/4 cup powdered sugar, firmly pressed into jar
1/3 cup brown sugar
1 3/4 cup chocolate chips placed in a zipper bag

Layer ingredients in order given in a 1 quart "wide mouth" canning jar. Press each layer firmly in place. Press the bag of chips into jar last, pressing it evenly on brown sugar layer. Give with instructions below.
See pgs. 4-5 for detailed instructions on layering and decorating jars.

Chocolate Peanut Butter Candy

1. Remove bag of chocolate chips from jar. Set aside.
2. Empty jar into a large bowl. Blend well.
3. Add: 3/4 stick butter or margarine, melted
             1 1/3 cups peanut butter
4. Mix until well blended. Press firmly into a 9" x 13" sprayed pan. (Wetting your hands helps.)
5. Place chocolate chips in a microsafe dish (discard plastic baggie first). Microwave on High 30 seconds, then stir well. Microwave at 15 second intervals, stirring well each time, until completely melted. Spread this chocolate over peanut butter layer.
6. Place in refrigerator for an hour to set. Cut into 1 1/2" squares - if it has been in the refrigerator, let it set out to soften before cutting.
   Store in refrigerator.

Makes 48 pieces.

Halloween Haystacks Mix in a Pint Jar

1 cup chocolate chips
1/2 cup flaked coconut colored orange with a drop
    each of yellow and red food coloring
3/4 cup chow mein noodles

Layer ingredients in order given in a 1 pint "wide mouth" canning jar. Press each layer firmly in place. Give with instructions below.

See pgs. 4-5 for detailed instructions on layering and decorating jars.

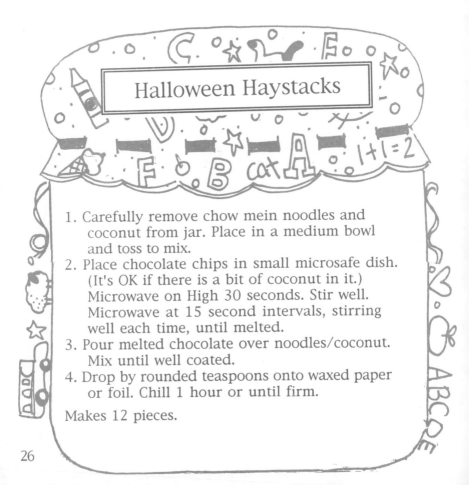

Halloween Haystacks

1. Carefully remove chow mein noodles and coconut from jar. Place in a medium bowl and toss to mix.
2. Place chocolate chips in small microsafe dish. (It's OK if there is a bit of coconut in it.) Microwave on High 30 seconds. Stir well. Microwave at 15 second intervals, stirring well each time, until melted.
3. Pour melted chocolate over noodles/coconut. Mix until well coated.
4. Drop by rounded teaspoons onto waxed paper or foil. Chill 1 hour or until firm.

Makes 12 pieces.

Popcorn Squares Mix in a Quart Jar
(Or Popcorn Balls)

3/4 cup M and M's® candies
3/4 cup salted or honey roasted peanuts
35 full size marshmallows (this is half a 10 oz. bag)
1/2 cup unpopped popcorn placed in a baggie

Layer ingredients in order given in a 1 quart "wide mouth" canning jar. Press each layer firmly in place. Wrap marshmallows securely with a square of plastic wrap. Press them in very firmly. Lay the bag of popcorn in last and use the lid of the jar to push it inside the jar. Give with instructions below.

See pgs. 4-5 for detailed instructions on layering and decorating jars.

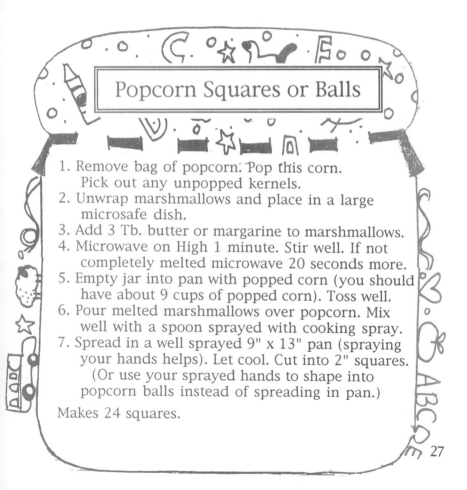

Popcorn Squares or Balls

1. Remove bag of popcorn. Pop this corn. Pick out any unpopped kernels.
2. Unwrap marshmallows and place in a large microsafe dish.
3. Add 3 Tb. butter or margarine to marshmallows.
4. Microwave on High 1 minute. Stir well. If not completely melted microwave 20 seconds more.
5. Empty jar into pan with popped corn (you should have about 9 cups of popped corn). Toss well.
6. Pour melted marshmallows over popcorn. Mix well with a spoon sprayed with cooking spray.
7. Spread in a well sprayed 9" x 13" pan (spraying your hands helps). Let cool. Cut into 2" squares. (Or use your sprayed hands to shape into popcorn balls instead of spreading in pan.)

Makes 24 squares.

Chex® Snack Mix in a Quart Jar

1/2 cup mixed salted nuts
1/2 cup broken small pretzels
1 cup Wheat Chex® cereal
1 cup Corn Chex® cereal
1 cup Rice Chex® cereal
1/2 tsp. seasoned salt
1/2 tsp. garlic powder

Layer ingredients in order given in a 1 quart "wide mouth" canning jar. Press each layer firmly in place. Sprinkle seasonings into jar on top of the mix. Give with instructions below.

See pgs. 4-5 for detailed instructions on layering and decorating jars.

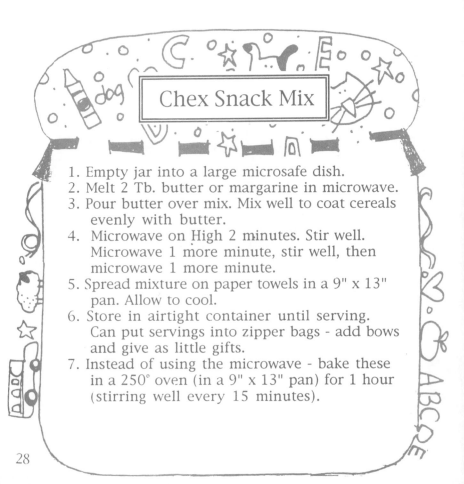

Chex Snack Mix

1. Empty jar into a large microsafe dish.
2. Melt 2 Tb. butter or margarine in microwave.
3. Pour butter over mix. Mix well to coat cereals evenly with butter.
4. Microwave on High 2 minutes. Stir well. Microwave 1 more minute, stir well, then microwave 1 more minute.
5. Spread mixture on paper towels in a 9" x 13" pan. Allow to cool.
6. Store in airtight container until serving. Can put servings into zipper bags - add bows and give as little gifts.
7. Instead of using the microwave - bake these in a 250° oven (in a 9" x 13" pan) for 1 hour (stirring well every 15 minutes).

Mix For Bird Treats in a Quart Jar

1 cup quick oats
1/3 cup brown sugar - pack tightly over oats
3/4 sunflower seeds in hulls (buy in pet food aisle of store)
1 cup small birdseed such as millet
3/4 cup cornmeal mixed with:
3/4 cups flour and placed in a zipper baggie

Layer ingredients in order given in a 1 quart "wide mouth" canning jar. Press each layer firmly in place. Give with instructions below.
See pgs. 4-5 for detailed instructions on layering and decorating jars.

Bird Treat

1. Empty all ingredients from jar into a large bowl.
2. Add: 1 cup peanut butter, smooth or crunchy
              1/2 cup water
3. Mix very well. Add more water if necessary to make a stiff dough. Spread in a 9" x 13" pan. Use a knife to score into 2" x 4" bars.
4. Bake at 250° for 20 minutes.
5. Leave in pan to cool. Cut into bars along scores. Feed birds with 1 bar. Keep remaining bars refrigerated until needed. This can be placed in a suet feeder if desired.

Makes 12 bars.

Granola Mix in a Quart Jar

1 cup oats
1 cup crisp rice cereal
1/2 cup brown sugar, pressing in very firmly
1/2 cup sliced almonds
1/2 cup wheat germ mixed with:
1 tsp. cinnamon
1/4 cup shelled sunflower seeds
3/4 cup raisins placed in a zipper baggie

Layer ingredients in order given in a 1 quart "wide mouth" canning jar. Press each layer firmly in place. Give with instructions below.

See pgs. 4-5 for detailed instructions on layering and decorating jars.

Granola

1. Remove bag of raisins. Set aside.
2. Empty jar into large bowl. Mix dry ingredients.
3. Add: 2 Tb. oil - Mix until well coated. Then add:
   1/3 cup honey - Mix very well.
4. Spread in a sprayed 9" x 13" pan.
5. Bake at 250° for 40 minutes - stir well after 20 minutes.
6. Allow to cool. Stir in raisins.
7. Store in airtight container or put individual servings into zipper bags.
8. Serve as a cereal with milk.

Mix For Granola Bars in a Quart Jar

1/2 cup honey roasted peanuts
1/3 cup brown sugar
1/4 cup flour
3 cups granola cereal (without raisins)

Layer ingredients in order given in a 1 quart "wide mouth" canning jar. Press each layer firmly in place. Give with instructions below.
See pgs. 4-5 for detailed instructions on layering and decorating jars.

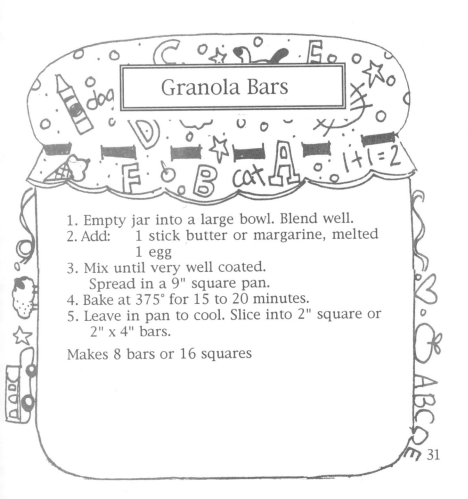

Granola Bars

1. Empty jar into a large bowl. Blend well.
2. Add: 1 stick butter or margarine, melted
             1 egg
3. Mix until very well coated.
   Spread in a 9" square pan.
4. Bake at 375° for 15 to 20 minutes.
5. Leave in pan to cool. Slice into 2" square or
   2" x 4" bars.

Makes 8 bars or 16 squares

Simple Snack Mix in a Pint Jar

Place following ingredients in a "wide-mouth" pint canning jar in this order:

1/4 cup M and M's® candies
1/2 cup honey roasted peanuts
1/4 cup raisins
1 cup Honey Nut Cheerios® cereal

Instructions for recipient:

Empty contents of jar into a serving bowl.
Toss to mix well.

Index